HOW TO TAKE A BULLET

AND OTHER SURVIVAL POEMS

HOW TO TAKE A BULLET

AND OTHER SURVIVAL POEMS

HOLLIE HARDY

For Alan

May you Survive!

Also: Happy Thanksgiving!

Hollie Hardy

2016

Punk ♥ Hostage ♥ Press
Hollywood, California

How to Take a Bullet
And Other Survival Poems

Hollie Hardy

Published by Punk ♥ Hostage ♥ Press

P.O. Box 1869
Hollywood, CA 90078
wp.punkhostagepress.com

ISBN-10: 1940213975
ISBN-13: 978-1-940213-97-2

Cover Art: Donald Morey
Cover Design: Donald Morey & Tom Madsen
Book Design & Layout: Hollie Hardy
Author Photo: Joe Carrow
Introduction: Toni Mirosevich
Editor: A. Razor

For Jason

EDITOR'S ACKNOWLEDGEMENTS

There are books that are out there, looking to be made, that are such profound extensions of the culmination of a writer's life and craft at an intersection that these books have a will to be made that is seemingly all their own. This book is one of those such books and the organic cultivation of its fruition is something we at Punk Hostage Press are excited to be a part of.

One day in an open patio of a humble beer garden on Telegraph Ave., SB Stokes was talking to A. Razor in regard to the editing of SB Stokes' book, *A History of Broken Love Things*. Hollie Hardy walked onto the patio, a co-conspirator of SB Stokes, in the seething cauldron of San Francisco Bay Area literary projects that have a vibrant significance in the local literary community.

Conversation quickly got around to books and SB Stokes mentioned a manuscript of merit that he had known Hollie Hardy to be working on for some time. A. Razor was shown the manuscript, which he proceeded to read right there while the conversation continued around him. He was so moved, he sent a copy to Iris Berry, who read it that evening and responded with a similar feeling...this is a book we would like to publish, by a writer who is immersed in the craft and dedicated to supporting the kind of community that creative efforts in wordsmithing could thrive in and inspire more works and community to grow.

This book is a simple demonstration of the capacity held within words as art, as works, as community, as family. It frames Hollie Hardy in a landscape of her own making, with physical laws that bend to her will, with an exposed vulnerability in her own heart, with a playful window onto souls we all hold in common. There is imagery packed into every line of every piece of work here, complimented by original artwork from Hollie's father, Donald Morey, a renowned artist in his own right.

Punk Hostage Press would like to acknowledge all the people in the literary community who have inspired, supported and even contributed to this book along the way to its being in your hands now. We want to thank Hollie Hardy for allowing Punk Hostage Press to publish this book that has had our attention from the first moment we read it. Our heartfelt gratitude to all of those who have supported our endeavors and made it possible for us to come across these organic intersections that would lead to this moment here and now.

We would also like to acknowledge the editors of these publications for previously publishing versions of the following titles:

The Common, "How to Jump From a Building into a Dumpster," and "How to Perform a Tracheotomy;" *The Common Online*, "How to Detangle a Bird Caught in Your Hair;" *Eleven Eleven*, "How to Survive a Riot," "How to Survive Adrift at Sea," "How to Survive If You are Buried Alive," and "How to Jump From a Bridge into a River;" *One Ded Cow*, "How to Escape When Tied Up;" *Parthenon West Review*, "How to Fend Off a Shark;" *A Sharp Piece of Awesome*, "How to Break Down a Door," "How to Survive an Earthquake," and "How to Take a Bullet;" *sPARKLE & bLINK*, "How to Land a Plane;" *Transfer*, "How to Control a Runaway Camel," "How to Survive When Lost in the Desert," "How to Survive an Avalanche," and "How to Treat Frostbite;" *The Velro Reader*, "How to Climb Out of a Well."

~A. Razor

AUTHOR'S NOTES & ACKNOWLEDGEMENTS

The poems in this collection have titles ruthlessly appropriated from *The Worst-Case Scenario Survival Handbook*. Between the lines of the literal, contemplative metaphors masquerade as instructions, invoking both survival and surrender. The landscape is often urban, woven of dream. Ocean wet and desert dry, here is a windswept city of powdered bone and liquid night. There is always the potential for desire. Teeth and sky. Blindfolds and breadcrumbs. Mouths naming and claiming the elements: fire, wind, texture, motion. There are dangerous beasts to conquer. Internal and external. Fear on lips and fingertips. These poems are weapons of change, lessons of smoke and rain, freedom, and finally, the breath.

This book, more than ten years in the making, would not exist without the love, support, feedback, encouragement, patience, and generosity of my fellow writers and professors, friends, family, editors, artists, and designers, to whom I offer my heartfelt gratitude.

Specifically, I would like to thank A. Razor and Iris Berry for liking the manuscript (and for claiming it for Punk Hostage). I would like to thank my creative writing professors at San Francisco State University: Toni Mirosevich, my brilliant and dedicated thesis advisor, who also retitled the book and wrote the introduction, Paul Hoover for teaching me how to cut, Truong Tran for inspiration, and Maxine Chernoff for giving the assignment that launched the very first "How To" poem in the collection.

Thank you to Nina Zolotow, Lori Savageau, and Annemarie Munn of the East Bay Lady Writers for their generous feedback, to SB Stokes for lighting the way to Punk Hostage, and to Camille T. Dungy, Jeannine Hall Gailey, John Hennessy, Paul Hoover, Major Jackson, Toni Mirosevich, and Chad Sweeney, for reading (and writing about) advanced copies of the book. Thanks to my dear friend Tom Madsen who dropped everything and went into work on his day off to complete the cover layout and design.

Thanks to my sister Little Erin Morey for listening long distance to every new poem I ever write. (Shout out to Taylor Morey and to Jessica Hardy for being awesome.) Love to Fred Clinton for being my biggest fan. Huge thanks to my mother, Susan Morey, for being so excited about my work, and for always believing in me and encouraging my desire to be a writer. Thanks Mom!

This book would be naked without my father, Donald Morey, who put everything in his own life on hold, and dedicated a month to drawing new original artwork for my book cover. Thanks for the art, Dad!

Finally, thank you to my amazing boyfriend, Jason Lujick, for his tireless love, patience, humor, sarcasm, and occasional sincerity. Also, for feeding me so well, and for stubbornly persisting in the flawed notion that poetry will one day make us rich. Love you.

~Hollie Hardy

INTRODUCTION

Toss out all the other "How To" books on your shelves. Those less than useful manuals on how to live a happy life, shod your horse, achieve nirvana in ten easy shake and bake steps. Replace with one shining new poetry book from Hollie Hardy.

How to Take a Bullet, And Other Survival Poems is part instruction manual, part poetic divination, part rumination of a visionary scout. The poems in this first collection not only teach you how to survive bullets and battles and boredom, but how to survive love, ennui, desire, and the slings and arrows of mates. You'll not only learn how to land a plane, but how to land a poem, not only how to treat a knife wound, but how to repair wounds less visible.

This poet takes you to an imaginative precipice and asks you to jump. As one line predicts, "...eventually you will land somewhere." Want to know how to survive a fall from that great height? Read this book. Hollie Hardy knows what you need to carry in your knapsack, beyond the potable water, a four-season tent, those pieces of flint. Packed in tight are poems that can sustain you through the most brutal winter or current climate crisis. With Hollie Hardy you couldn't want for a better girl guide.

~Toni Mirosevich, author of *The Takeaway Bin*
and *Pink Harvest: Tales of Happenstance*

TABLE OF CONTENTS

Revising the Mountain: Tricks for Traveling Alone

THE LANTERN SEA

INSTRUCTIONS FOR BREATHING

HOW TO SURVIVE ADRIFT AT SEA

There are handprints all over your weekends
Windows thrown wide to the night
The curve of loneliness
Renders strange fingers
Brushing your bare shoulder

You concoct an elixir of fire
Goldfish swim below the surface of sleep

Unfurling the lantern sea
Until you can't stop dreaming the wet of it

You savor the sensation of drowning
Instead of writing

An impossible crush unfastens
Something that was neatly folded

Paper-thin panties hit the floor
Dissolve into mint ice cream

The fragrance of another Wednesday night

But desire is never permanent
And something new inflates your lungs
Vacating old beliefs

In the nick of time
In the nick of bone
In the bed of another lesson
In the unspoken

Miles are traveled

And with these scissors
You can mend the holes

HOW TO FEND OFF A SHARK

Wet fists in your eyes. The thump of undrumming
A figure in your peripheral vision

Here is the rind of night. Facing off on a rock of ice
Nightgown whipping, ragged around your thighs

Because silence is an expression of fear
Unwave that flag, unsmoke that cigarette
Unfuck that friend
These desperate little fistfuls of defiance

This jazz song does not belong to you
Warm, the sensation of sleep. Threadbare
The quality of wishing

Because police are at the door again
This wrecking ball in your bedroom
This fresh fountain of silver in your hair

Blue, the function of smoke. Rumpled
The flavor of resistance

There are things that vanish unexpectedly
The stone talisman you carried for luck
Photographs burned in a fire
Bewildered, the pillow of regret

Because our experiences overlap. Bodies at rest
Hoarding dreams like stolen rainwater

HOW TO GET TO THE SURFACE
IF YOUR SCUBA TANK RUNS OUT OF AIR

You are alone in the cool black of the deep
This silent alien landscape

You are moving slowly
You stop, to twist the strings

Your lungs are antique elevators inside wrought iron cages
Everything that happens

Keeps on being
A beginning

Break up your own little tedium
Fight with fists or feet or bottles or knives

Imagine you are walking along the dusk
Across a paper skyline

Through the narrow streets of a port
Where the air smells of salt and newsawn lumber

Endlessly sustain the discourse of your lover's absence
Reset your circadian rhythms

Persist in dutiful, discreet, conformist delirium
Tamed and banalized by literature

Blend the stiff and the supple
Think of flies entering a closed mouth

Recall the night of your birth
You don't need an audience

To practice routines that tell your body
Bedtime approaches

Eventually you will fall asleep
Corroded by the transmission of narrative

Write a transparent calligraphy
It's like being twice as asleep

HOW TO TREAT FROSTBITE

You live inside an old photograph of yourself
A frozen wind chime rusting

Where did you go wrong on this river road?
How did you become so lonely?

You trace the outline of bones
As your body evolves
A few steps closer to unraveling

Fold the days around you like a silk robe
Scratch at the skin of dailyness

In the empty afterness
Imagine a mango light

Wipe your sarcasm on your jeans
And punch a tiny hole in the center of the sky

Roll the morning around under your tongue
Like a jaw breaker, testing its smoothness

Weaving the hours into a nest
Find old scraps to stitch to the new

The angle of repose
Is something that never happened

A sky gallops across your brow
You are asleep in your bed

On fire
In the winter of your history lesson

HOW TO BREAK DOWN A DOOR

1.

Determine the nature of the door

Begin by reexamining everything you hold to be true

This baggage you carry

This egg you hold behind your back

Where did it come from? To whom does it belong?

2.

Stand at the threshold

Run your fingers over the cool metal bars

The brass knocker

The hollow splintering wood

Press your ear against the door

Recognize the sound of the ocean

Ships at a distance have every man's wish on board

3.

Imagine a field of wild flowers

Yellow, purple, orange

Scent of childhood summers

Fresh-cut grass

A breeze unbuckles your hair

4.

Imagine strolling the wide sidewalks of a foreign city
Ancient ornate buildings infuse you with wonder
The market place buzzes with color
A symphony of voices

5.

Enter the subway bound for anywhere
Your passport in your pocket
A small smile on your lips
Life shrinks or expands in proportion to your courage

6.

Make a list of things you love
Sticky sweet of mango
Wet sand between your toes
Sunshine settling in your eyelashes
Your lover's hand resting in the small of your back

7.

Throw away the rules of physics
You are standing outside the world
Peeking in through the keyhole
The door disappears
This moment is your life

HOW TO CURE INSOMNIA

Braid your fears into a cord
Something you can bite down on

Fill in the cracks of missing memories
With little bones

Swaddled in your urban sanctuary
You've forgotten the purpose of night

Abandon the hum of city, howl of homeless
White-hot lights and hipster-chic shadows

Let your mind ride out
Beyond the florescent metropolis
Where street lamps fade into farms

Reach for the black edge of ocean

Notice
There is no moon

NAMING YOUR CAMEL

STRATEGIES FOR DATING

HOW TO JUMP FROM A BUILDING
INTO A DUMPSTER

Come home from a Tupperware party
Look out across the lake and imagine the feel of your
Tongue, against the truth

Prevent the neighbor's dog from barking
Try to find the unselfconsciously erotic person
Hiding within

Refuse to exist sanely under conditions of absolute reality
Be the old man carrying flowers on his head
Be life-like

Think of asking the servants to wax the change
Before placing it in the Chinese tank
You keep on your dresser

Penetrate impenetrable curtains of possibility
Smooth the silken, sad, uncertain rustling of
Each purple curtain

Eat this place. Eat men like air

Force yourself to function
Far below the summit of your potential
Like a potato that never entirely cooled

Learn how to jump. Jump straight down.

Consider the mindless tosspot of random chance

Take a snapshot of a young woman
Standing in front of a parked motorcycle

When the war is over, go no place in particular

After the monkeys come down from the trees
Teach them to hurl sharp objects

If ink is the blood of language, and paper is its flesh
Don't believe the official report. Wear it like a mask

Always answer, "Oh yes!"

Try the edge of the Viking's little ax with your fingers
Tell lies about parrots in a colorless singsong

Just stand there, looking at the sky
Or the glove's twisted finger

Because it is difficult to throw out anything
So precise and crafted as a metal key
Throw something out of a window

Buy a box of Froot Loops
Feed the Froot Loops to your gerbil
Buy four cups of coffee and a six pack of Jolt
Accuse the Church of building green masturbation toilets
Be consumed by unreason. Stare at an empty glass of milk

Accessorize with a necklace of teeth
Reveal the bite marks on your shoulder

Tighten the circles of love like a noose
squeezing, ripping, slicing

Let your spirit into the kitchen
Teach yourself how to breathe
Take risks with mustard

Be a tattered billboard for someone else's reality

Sometimes in a flash
Wake up and reverse the direction of your fall

Start a subtle fire beneath my skin
Decide not to put on the underwear
Don't let the five dollars tempt you

Use a hard vocabulary to contain the terrible softness

Don't leave! I haven't come yet!

Remember:

It's just a screen door

HOW TO PERFORM A TRACHEOTOMY

The first thing you need to know is that the tracheotomy
is an act of desperation and/or violence that should only
be committed when there is no other option.

SOME CIRCUMSTANCES WHEN IT MIGHT BE
NECESSARY TO PERFORM A TRACHEOTOMY:

The victim is choking on a thin mint
and is unresponsive to the "hind-lick" maneuver

The victim is your lover and he/she has disappointed you
by eating the last Girl Scout cookie

The victim wrote "Bitch" on the side of your car
with a sharpie

The victim has an irritating, high-pitched voice or
a British accent

The victim is a stranger that fell in front of a bus
wearing shoes you could never afford

WHAT YOU WILL NEED:

A razor blade, knife, scissors, or hammer

A straw, a pen, or a stale Red Vine®

There will not be time for sterilization of your tools, so
don't bother. Infection is the least of your worries.

HOW TO PROCEED:

1. Kneel over the victim and whisper:
   Do you know what you've done to deserve this?

2. Move your finger about one inch down the neck
   until you feel a bulge

3. Seize the tool of your choosing, and grasp it
   with both hands high above your head

4. Aim for the bulge and be brave

5. Insert the breathing straw into the bloody hole

6. If you have done the procedure correctly
   you should be able to remove the victim's shoes

7. Run away

HOW TO GET A JOB
YOU'RE NOT QUALIFIED FOR

You are a boat lost under the hair of coves

Water penetrates your pinewood hull

Wash clean the bluish wine-stains and splashes of vomit

Dream of the green night of the dazzled snows

Take away from God his sound

Clack your metal wings

Play a tune on a tinny piano in someone else's house

Breathe into the alphabet you find upon a chair

Dim the towed rock

Twang the rushed snow

Bite the nut-like substance

Destroy love's life-giving vulgarity

Flutter up from the center of the track

Amidst the pink flamingoes

Consider Lana Turner's collapse

Apologize to the sun

Feign a great calm

Say there is money but it rusted

Say the time of moon is not right for escape

Dream of telling a man to be precise
Spread like the shadow of knowledge
Over a sleeping person
Expose a utopian desire with seasonal corners and
Nondeciduous oaks
Do not take the job seriously, since it is in the past
Do not be sentient
Avoid using plots, characters
Or the language of Shakespeare

Like a fluid that whaps against the walls of the jar
Work within the machine of the culture
Stand in your kitchen and stare at the honey bear's face
Like a shattered boat of a person

In the bright light of shipwreck, the bones of fish
The roots of words

Echo like history
Tear at the grass with your alien small teeth

Hunt by camera
Vote in the pouches of twilight

Seem to row in one lake and sail on the other

Be the impossible woman, the fickle luster, the chimera
Turned to salt
Craft a way forward
Play any role you like and go on forever

Spring up like unknown, unnamed
Vegetables in the patch
Remember the breath, the hammer, the syllable, the ear
The heart and the line

Declare war on Bolivia
Pluck wings off butterflies
Take back everything you've ever said
History will absolve you

Wish you were an apple seed
Wish Joan Baez was here singing "Tears of Rage"
Wander around with a ladder and a bucket
Keep combing your hair

Go back to being a cannibal

Sit by a volcano

Wrap yourself in an opalescent carapace of fog

Drink nothing but your mother's milk

Aimlessly pound the shore

Develop scar-tissue

Sleep with all of the people in the poems

At 35, throw away your crutches

Flop around in the water

Instead of courting the ugly queen

Stand against the crumbling wall of the fort

To enjoy an orgasm in the public void

Hold back the desire to be named

Grow crows instead of hands, to explain

Your difficult childhood

Arrange your crotch

Say "I love you," but avoid eye contact

Don't grab me by my arm!
I don't like my arm being grabbed

To get this job, you must bring back archeology
This is why we have storage

HOW TO DETANGLE A BIRD
CAUGHT IN YOUR HAIR

First you have to have hair
This trend toward baldness negates the problem

Once you have grown a luscious mane
Gather images on your lion tongue

Ripe peaches, sizzle of bacon
Crisp campfire scent of an almost winter night
Handful of rain or feathers or marbles
Details of sunset, sand and fast cars

Weave your materials carefully
Remember that birds like shiny things

The colors and flavors you choose
May affect the type of bird you can lure
Into your hair-nest

It helps to know what you're looking for
The hummingbird is popular due to its size
And general friendliness

The swan is elegant but angry
Loons, pelicans and ostriches
Are obviously to be avoided

With patience, you will eventually find
A bird snarled in your hair

It might not be the bird you initially had in mind
But give it some time, this one might surprise you

Protect your eyes and face
As you attempt to pet the iridescent feathers
Of your albatross or owl

Avoid wearing a hat

In the event that you tire of this entanglement
the following options are available:

1. Tenderly cut the bird away, like a piece of gum
   from a child's hair

2. Start a small fire on the back of your head
   and begin to run

HOW TO CONTROL A RUNAWAY CAMEL

Name your camel Alexander the Great,
Charlie, Honey Baby, or Cherry-Apple-
Bend-Over-Surprise

Ownership begins with a name

Wrap your legs around the beast and dig
Your fingers into the brittle earth of its mane
Coarse as a tongue

Learn how to say yes, and no

Pay attention to the motion of sea
In your hands. Dry, folding
And folded, as a paper bird

Say to yourself: practice makes permanent

Your camel reeks of damp
Socks and urine, leftover laundry
After you fall out of love

Never tell Charlie where you are going

Remember, the ride is just a game
You must chase the one who runs
Run from those who chase

HOW TO SLIP AWAY UNNOTICED

You are a feast of vision
A body of land

A high-heeled
Insect of night

With rogue
And monstrous tongue

Your hem
Unravels in flight

Slice loose threads
Crisp and mean

Scorched wing of flesh
Sweats your seam

Wrapped in wilted patchwork
Of this unfragrant bloom

Your dress changes colors
As you glide from room to room

A CLOSET FULL OF SCISSORS

WEAPONS FOR CHANGE

HOW TO LEAVE A TRAIL FOR RESCUERS
IF YOU ARE LOST IN THE WILDERNESS

Leave your fingernails behind in the dirt
Scatter clumps of hair in the breeze
A gently sliced Achilles
Will paint your footprints daintily

Let the wind take your clothes
Like an old song about endings
Lie back in your bed of leaves

Let the night insects bite
And sting your naked flesh
Stay awake and wait for me

I'd fall for you, he said, if you were in trouble
I'm a sucker for a damsel in distress

The day turns burnt evening then midnight
A navy blue forest appears

Glistening slices of moon
Splash through the lattice of leaves
Silhouettes of wind, damp with possibility

Your dress might flutter
If it were a dress

Your fingers find the textures of trees
Barefoot in moist earth, a guidebook in Braille

Somewhere, the sound of the river
Rolls over and over itself

HOW TO JUMP FROM A BRIDGE INTO A RIVER

Survey the melted sherbet horizon
of the city at sunset
as seen from the bridge
over silver blue water

Buildings in silhouette
glitter the fading day
adorned with the festive glow
of light pollution

Not a Christmas tree
strung with white lights
festooned with ornaments
and myrrh-scented presents

But a carnival at dusk
when the Ferris wheel first comes to life
and the smell of popcorn butters the air
jaunty music unchains its eerie charm

When children are filled
with cotton candy and wonder
because they haven't yet realized
that there is no Santa

The river winks and nods
and reaches for your hand
you can see yourself reflected
in its wet black eyes

Savor the evening's last moments
with each breath of sky
the river summons
your slow freefall into night

HOW TO AVOID
BREAKING THROUGH THE ICE

The trick is to glide
across the surface of life
like children skating a winter pond
mittened hands clasped
cheeks and noses pink with cold
hearts pumping exertion, exhilaration
as round and round they rush
avoiding the weak edges
threatening to break
open like thunder and
plunge you into the deep

A light snow falls
flakes settle unnoticed on eyelashes
a fresh glaze of white erasing
slim lines of barren forest
the silent hawk circling
brushstrokes against the sky

In the distance a curl of smoke
grays the air above your home
but you do not think
of your mother
chopping wood, building the fire
working nights at the factory
You do not think of your father
somewhere far away, trying to sketch
your face in his notebook
realizing he can no longer conjure
your image, turning instead
to the waitress, drawing the curve
of her neck, the line of her hip, her apron

She is unaware of the secret
growing inside her
somewhere beneath
the slippery surface
in the frigid dark
where life moves
at its own pace

HOW TO SURVIVE AN EARTHQUAKE

~For Haiti, January 12, 2010

As the sun rises over tents
of sticks and tarps
your breath snags
on jagged edges
begins to unravel

Orphans wander
in search of mothers
dust caked gray
in open wounds

In the rumbling aftermath
below the baseline
moans of horror
muffle cries for help

Desperation breeds thieves
rape waits in shadows
one hundred thousand dead
your city aches in ashes

Hands press together in prayer
missing hands
empty hands

hands holding hands
hands reaching for hope

Husband cries for wife
his voice a siren
his bare feet soaked
in blood, he squats

In the wreckage
of his life
cradles your head
waits for an angel

HOW TO NAVIGATE A MINE FIELD

The pen, the page
These weapons of change

These agents of inertia, of insurrection
Of your voice

Like the slow motion of snow melt
Sculpting a new landscape

As the flower of our times
Nods whitening

You locate change in abandonment
Mine the body's oceans

The moon's slow tidings
Churning with blood and sand

Blinded by the glare of culture
You attend to your dailiness

Remember the lessons of history
Old news tied to the feet of birds

Once-urgent messages
Driven on the backs of beasts

News of revolution, news of change
Of new kinds of freedom

Or half empty
The change of new oppression

Another silent story
Embedded in the subtext

Of the disappeared
Of murdered journalists

Grandmothers marching in plazas
And children burning to ash

While we build new bridges, buy new phones
The dim threat of apocalypse unheeded

You execute change in the trenches
Alive with resistance

Minding the power of rocks
To bend the blood

HOW TO TAKE A BULLET

The wind is loud and deliberate
Like big brothers
And trucks on the highway

It brings the dark
Odor of low tide
Blows a black fog into the hills

Where it settles in
Like a foreign occupation
Erases the contours of horizon

Trees whisper and sway
Tap nervous fingers
Against glass houses

A train hurries by
Its whistle a wail
A fleeting moan

A mother
On the anniversary
Of her son's death

You are on your knees
Curled into yourself
Rocking, singing

His uniform pressed
To your cheek
Like a blankie

HOW TO START A FIRE WITHOUT MATCHES

In the Never Never Land
Of your outstretched hand

In the blistering menace
Without rain to wash your days

Armies march
To the bureaucratic clack
Of keyboards

Whose nimble fingers bid
On eBay's auction guns
Procure the cheapest
Amazon bombs

Headlines demonize
The oppressed
The unemployed
The working

While you sit smug
In your grim naïveté

Squabbling over issues
Invented as distractions

While apples and oil
Drive your country

Like a jet plane
Into flames

HOW TO SURVIVE A RIOT

~For Oscar Grant (1986 - 2009)

Begin by living in Oakland
Near the urban center

Become a casual observer
Of racial injustice

Watch a white cop shoot
An unarmed black man
In the back
On the news
Over and over

Watch the crowd gather
Storm clouds in the city center
Ready to tear apart
In protest

To loot burn destroy
Their own city
For justice

Or
Injustice

Board up your windows
Turn out the lights
Hold your breath

The mother cries
Murder!
When the verdict comes down—
Involuntary manslaughter
Two to four years
Then the killer goes free

We will avenge you
With our bodies (arrest us!)
We will get drunk and rap
About truth

We will break your windows!
We will fuck up your car!
Riot on your porch!
Shit in your yard!

This. Is. Protest!

Lock your vehicles and cover them with tarps
Hoping to render them invisible

Convene with your neighbors on the roof
Like victims of a flood waiting to be rescued

Watch the flash mob burgeon
In front of your home
Listen to the kaleidoscope of sound—

Shrill discord of car alarms
Sirens wailing kids shouting
Crackbang of fireworks
Dogs barking unseen bells ringing
Someone pounding a dumpster
With a metal pipe or a ball bat
News choppers beat the air

Smoke bombs cloud the sky, fires—
Bright orange and soot black
Smolder in garbage cans

Kids parade on foot and on bicycles
Black bandanas cover faces like bandits
Running laughing drinking

Protest!

Lemmings climbing your gate

Protest!

They see you watching but don't care

Protest!

Nothing makes a town more beautiful
Than boarded up windows
Sidewalks sparkling with blood and glass

On Channel 4, the local news shows
Hundreds of police in riot gear
Marching down Broadway
Like martial law

Cheer as they swoop in
To clear the vandals
From your lawn, then

Silence.

Remember Oscar Grant

REVISING THE MOUNTAIN

TRICKS FOR TRAVELING ALONE

HOW TO FOIL A UFO ABDUCTION

Become a child

with a clock

radio controlled

car or computer

and screwdriver

to dismantle

take apart

unfurl

rip open

and peer inside

a heart

(or) your own mind

to see how

it works

HOW TO SURVIVE IF YOU ARE BURIED ALIVE

Sit down by the window's heartbeat

to listen for rain

fingertips brush the body as Braille

seeking cracks in the façade

or an egress

from this book of wind

breath recurs often

brazen as the north star

a test of endurance

through layers of weather

how many stones are required

to collapse a lung

or a desire

HOW TO JUMP FROM A MOVING TRAIN

Track tied
Your childhood

Blossoms
Behind you

Wet lashes
Petals of memory

Only motion
Guides you

Your hands consumed
By thunder

New breath
Unchains your flesh

You are earth-stained
Sparrow stealing flight

HOW TO SURVIVE IF YOUR PARACHUTE FAILS TO OPEN

In the minute eternity

Before the skydive

Before the parachute opens

With a blast of wind and color

And the ground rushes up

There is

This writhing chaos

This tumultuous heartbeat

A floating moment

When you wonder

If you will really jump

And you wonder if

You already have

HOW TO SURVIVE WHEN LOST IN THE DESERT

In the crackling aftermath
Become a liquid

When your lovers try to hold you
Run blithely through their fingers

Evaporate

The mirage will expand
Pulled from crooked mouths

Against the stolen panoply of sky
Become content with the memory

Of your wetness
On their hands and lips

HOW TO WRESTLE FREE FROM AN ALLIGATOR

As your hangover
Settles

Around you
Like confetti

Claw at the triage
Of your infinite to-do list

Let your snarl slide
Down around your ankles

This beast
Must be put to bed

A light flicks on
In the doorway

Wind whips irony
Like strands of hair

Your canines
Calloused

Your eyes
Unblinking

HOW TO SURVIVE AN AVALANCHE

Using only your keyboard
trace the outline of the woman
you've always wanted to be

When you find yourself filling in
the hair, the scales, the sharp
sharp teeth

Let the sky bleed
into the margins of
this burgeoning narrative
this dirty white noise, this media drift

Let her blind grope find you
in the dark
these paper soft fingertips

Threadbare and alone
accumulating snow
with wet red edges

HOW TO SMOKE A CIGAR

Rough the edges
Steamy as gravel

Your voice
Smoke blue

Graphite soft
A rain-slicked city

Focus your mouth
The lips are key

Unhinge your wicked
Daydreams

Let your teeth
Graze

And your breath
Breathe

Head back
Adjust your hat

Your heat
A small fever

Beating like a sun

Stained fingers taste
Tobacco and earth

Tiny lessons
Of adulthood

Your journey
Maps the body

Unfurling its ghosts
Shadow ballerinas

Twirling for no one

HOW TO FIND YOUR WAY
WITHOUT A COMPASS

Invisible fingerprints paint
Your body a jungle, humming

Follow whispered directions
To trace the unfamiliar path

You, the stranger
Your life, an odyssey

Feel your way in the dark
Across the cotton landscape

The stone strain
Of muscles

Slows your pace
Until every nerve awakens

Become the fire
Revising the mountain

Always in search of fuel

HOW TO CLIMB OUT OF A WELL

If the jug breaks
It brings misfortune

You are the distant pebble
Echoing

Ignore the ripe wet pain
Spring up like light, lubricating

Remember
The electricity of boys

Muscular and savage
This itch of bones

Distant circle of white
The sky, another lifetime

A fleeting after-image
This empty grasp

He who throws himself away
Is no longer sought by others

Go ahead
Drink the poison

You are ancient here

HOW TO TAKE A PUNCH

Your days are bunched fists and blindfolds
Waiting for a siren to signal some release

When you leave you keep moving
Sharpen your hands in shadows
Suck out the venom, cross against the light
Withhold the flutter of your big sad eyes

Pieces of you drop away
Like bread crumbs, black butterflies
Your dress unravels, and then your skin

Threadbare, you reach for the same pattern
Tear another organ from your body
And begin again

HOW TO ESCAPE WHEN TIED UP

No one can know
Your unpronounceable name
Raw skin and chapped hands
Measure the power of invisibility

This is your country now
Tapestry of lost ambitions
Pale as dust on the surface
Of someone else's bed

Turn your eyes upward
To let shadows crawl
Across ceiling cracks
The soft accents of bondage

There's something about the texture
Of this burlap landscape
Its loose weave lets in rain
And the rough hands of men

HOW TO TREAT A BULLET OR KNIFE WOUND

~For Lee Miller (1907- 1977)

Take off your gown
Finger the trigger
Reclaim
The curve of your neck
A smooth white dove
Your elegant hands
Disembodied
Your severed breasts
Dismembered, defiant
Ready for the feast

Walk backwards
Down stairs
And into mouths
Into arms full of
Objects
Splintered glass
Lilies and moon shadows
These words about love

The dead sleep in your arms
With pretty white teeth

And on the pages of journals
The texture of bondage is a bell jar
A trophy of light
Birdcage, banjo
Shadow of a saw
Shrouded in mesh and lace
Stripped, repurposed, recombined, reloaded
Man carves his name
In the crook of your eyelid

You are the statue, you are the breath
Restless and ricochet, iron and silk

In a landscape of drowned mouths
Where shells burst near snow
In a train full of bodies
In the symphony of war
Smell the charred wet wood
Carry the blood, the bones, the bottle
These photos, your legacy of friendship
Your necklace of loneliness

HOW TO LAND A PLANE

It's the small things that hold us
Handcuffs and leftover puzzle pieces
Names like fences that keep us home

Always the stories are about freedom
How to disentangle, how to unglue

You are a kite on a frayed string. You are breakfast
Every morning. You are the voice of your mother
Quietly unscrewing the light bulb

You are the dog, barking at strangers and skateboards
The city still beats at the heart of you

But the music of longing is melancholy
How can this grasping gesture reconcile
The notion of impermanence?

The door is open and you can see
The bright invitation of sun and sky

You are drawn to motion
Like leaves unwinding the wind

Eventually you will land somewhere

NOTES

All of the poems in this collection have titles appropriated from Joshua Piven and David Borgenich, *The Complete Worst-Case Scenario Survival Handbook* (1999 - 2007).

"Ships at a distance have every man's wish on board" is from Zora Neale Hurston, *Their Eyes Were Watching God*.

"Life shrinks or expands in proportion to your courage" is from Anaïs Nin, *The Diary of Anaïs Nin*, Volume 3.

"This moment is your life" is attributed to Omar Khayyám.

"Your lungs are antique elevators inside wrought iron cages" is from Maxim Jakubowski, "The K.C. Suite," *The Mammoth Book of Erotica* (2000).

"Fight with fists, with feet, with bottles or knives," "dusk across a paper skyline," and "through the narrow streets of a port where the air smells of salt and newsawn lumber," are appropriated or paraphrased from Cormac McCarthy, *Blood Meridian: Or The Evening Redness in the West*.

"Endlessly sustain the discourse of your lover's absence," and "Persist in dutiful, discreet, conformist delirium, tamed and banalized by literature" are from Roland Barthes, *A Lover's Discourse: Fragments*.

"Flies Enter a Closed Mouth" is the English translation of

"Por boca cerrada entran las moscas" Pablo Neruda, *Pablo Neruda: Five Decades: A Selection (Poems: 1925-1970)*, trans. Ben Belitt.

"You don't need an audience to practice routines that tell your body bedtime approaches" is from Mireille Guilliano, *French Women Don't Get Fat: The Secret of Eating for Pleasure*.

"Write a transparent calligraphy" is from Rumi, "Two Days of Silence," *Rumi the Book of Love: Poems of Ecstasy and Longing*, trans. Coleman Barks.

"It's like being twice as asleep" is from Geoffrey Dyer, "11," *The Dirty Halo of Everything*.

"Come home from a Tupperware party" is from Thomas Pynchon, *The Crying of Lot 49*.

"Imagine the feel of your tongue against the truth" is from Tim O'Brien, *In the Lake of the Woods*.

"Prevent the neighbor's dog from barking" is from W.H. Auden, "Funeral Blues."

"Try to find the unselfconsciously erotic person hiding within" is from Carol Queen, *Exhibitionism for the Shy*.

"Refuse to exist sanely under conditions of absolute reality" is from Shirley Jackson, *The Haunting of Hill House.*

"Old man carrying flowers on his head" is from ee cummings, "Suppose."

"Think of asking the servants to wax the change before placing it in the Chinese tank you keep on your dresser" is from David Sedaris, *Naked.*

"Penetrate impenetrable curtains of possibility" is from Leonard Cohen, *Beautiful Losers.*

"The silken, sad, uncertain rustling of each purple curtain" is from Edgar Allan Poe, "The Raven."

"Eat men like air" is from Sylvia Plath, "Lady Lazarus."

"Function far below the summit of your potential," "like a potato that never entirely cooled," "the mindless tosspot of random chance," "after the monkeys come down from the trees teach them to hurl sharp objects," and "if ink is the blood of language, and paper is its flesh" are paraphrased from Tom Robbins, *Villa Incognito.*

"Jump straight down" is one of the real instructions from Joshua Piven and David Borgenich, "How to Jump from a Building into a Dumpster," *The Worst-Case Scenario Survival Handbook.*

"A snapshot of a young woman standing in front of a parked motorcycle," "When the war is over, go no place in particular," and "Use a hard vocabulary to contain the terrible softness" are from Tim O'Brien, *The Things They Carried.*

"Try the edge of the Viking's little ax with your fingers" is from Jörgen Moe, "Viggo and Beate" *The Birch and the Star: And Other Stories* (1915), trans. Gudrun Thorne-Thomsen.

"Tell lies about parrots in a colorless singsong," "Just stand there, looking at the sky" and "the glove's twisted finger" are from Virginia Woolf, *To the Lighthouse.*

"It is difficult to throw out anything so precise and crafted as a metal key" is from Leonard Cohen, *The Favorite Game.*

"Buy a box of Froot Loops. Feed the Froot Loops to your gerbil" and "Buy four cups of coffee and a six pack of Jolt" are from Larry Berger, Manek Mistry, and Paul Rossi, "The Froot Loops Technique," *Up Your Score* (1987).

"Accuse the Church of building green masturbation toilets," "consumed by unreason," "stare at an empty glass of milk," "tighten the circles of love like a noose, squeezing, ripping, slicing," "let your spirit into the kitchen," "taking risks with mustard," and "tattered billboard for reality" are appropriated or paraphrased from Leonard Cohen, *Beautiful Losers*.

"Start a subtle fire beneath my skin" is from Sappho, quoted in Roland Barthes, *A Lover's Discourse: Fragments*.

"There will not be time for sterilization of your tools, so do not bother. Infection is the least of your worries" and "Move your finger about one inch down the neck until you feel a bulge" are real instructions from Joshua Piven and David Borgenich, "How to Treat Frostbite," *The Worst-Case Scenario Survival Handbook*.

Each stanza of "How to Get a Job You're Not Qualified For" contains lines appropriated or paraphrased from poems by the following poets, respectively: Arthur Rimbaud, John Weiners, Barbara Guest, Frank O'Hara, Lorine Niedecker, Lyn Hejinian, Leslie Scalapino, Eileen Myles, George Oppen, Kathleen Fraser, Rae Armantrout, Sharon Olson, Nicanor Parra, Robert Creeley, Elaine Equi, Jack Spicer, Carla Harryman, C.A. Conrad, Fernando Pessoa, and Renee Gladman.

"Where shells burst near snow" is from Lee Miller, WWII war correspondence, Alsace campaign.

HOLLIE HARDY can teach you how to survive anything. She is an adjunct English instructor at Berkeley City College and lecturer at San Francisco State University, where she received a Master of Fine Arts in Poetry. An active participant in the local Bay Area literary scene, Hardy co-hosts the popular monthly reading series, Saturday Night Special, An East Bay Open Mic. She is one of the founders of the annual Beast Crawl Literary Festival in Oakland, curator of Litquake's Flight of Poets, and a former Editor-in-Chief of *Fourteen Hills: The SFSU Review*. Her work has appeared in *The Common, Eleven Eleven, Milvia Street, One Ded Cow, Parthenon West Review, A Sharp Piece of Awesome, sPARKLE & bLink, Transfer,* and other journals. She lives in Oakland, California. www.holliehardy.com

PRAISE FOR HOW TO TAKE A BULLET
AND OTHER SURVIVAL POEMS

With wit and candor, Hollie Hardy writes for her life. "Break up your own little tedium," these poems remind us. With their riffs on existing literature and recurrent crises, Hardy's poems show us what can be gained from trying old tricks in new ways. Hardy shows us how to survive a life lived just over the edge. These poems are playful in the way tussling wolf cubs are playful. They are physical and practical. They are recognizing and revealing strength.

~Camille T. Dungy, author of *Smith Blue* and
What to Eat, What to Drink, What to Leave for Poison

Hollie Hardy's "Survival Poems" teach us to remain whole by being multiple, to live inside our paradoxes in a "symphony of voices," to take a bullet by merging its motion into a continuous act of self-invention, to "enjoy an orgasm in the public void" and to "use a hard vocabulary to contain the terrible softness." If Munch's "Scream" embodies the anxiety of urban Modernity, Hollie Hardy's SHOUT unlocks a music to celebrate all this speed, all this contradiction, arriving toward a new super-Self in both multiplication and recovery, in protest and love. In the fullest sense of the word, your survival may depend on reading this book!

~Chad Sweeney, author of *Wolf's Milk* and
The Parable of Hide and Seek

A sensuous and persistent vision defines Hollie Hardy's *How to Take a Bullet*, one that sees our age of self-help and DIY culture as an aesthetic vehicle for more ritualistic and artful remakings of the self in language and hip codes. Some fires actually do revise the mountains. Here is one.

~Major Jackson, author of *Holding Company,* and *Hoops*

Hollie Hardy's jaw-dropping book of poems, *How to Take a Bullet,* brilliantly expands the "how to" model of expression to include the impossible. What exactly would be required to take a bullet well, a deft last-minute turn or full-frontal acceptance? In "How to Survive If Your Parachute Fails to Open," we have the perfect model of the Zen of recklessness: "A floating moment / when you wonder / if you will really jump / and you wonder if / you already have." The Latin poet Horace famously wrote that poetry should "both delight and instruct." The delight of *How to Take a Bullet* is not in the book's moral imperatives (though it is savagely wise), but rather in the striking humor and incisiveness of its lines: "Wrap yourself in an opalescent carapace of fog / Drink nothing but your mother's milk." We abandon ourselves to the craft of "the green night of the dazzled snows" and how to "remove the victim's shoes."

~Paul Hoover, author of *Desolation: Souvenir,* and editor of *Postmodern American Poetry*

Exhilarating and entertaining, Hollie Hardy's *How to Take a Bullet, And Other Survival Poems* takes you on a journey to invulnerability, with instructive poems that teach you how to survive a parachute failure, wrestle alligators, or build a fire. Full of "acts of desperation and/or violence," Hardy's fierce first book will grab you by the throat (sometimes literally, as in "How to Perform a Tracheotomy") and won't let you go.

~Jeannine Hall Gailey, author of *She Returns to the Floating World,* and *Becoming the Villainess*

How to Take a Bullet will keep you safe—and stimulated. Satisfied. Strap it on, reader; it's better than a bulletproof vest, a shot of whiskey, and an EpiPen combined. With sly echoes of Poe, Woolf, Nin, Plath, McCarthy, Neruda, and Barthes, it'll protect, tranquilize, reanimate, and reinvigorate. And then there's that edge of menace and comedy that's all Hardy's own. Submit to it, my friend.

~John Hennessy, author of of *Coney Island Pilgrims* and poetry editor for *The Common*

MORE TITLES FROM PUNK HOSTAGE PRESS

Fractured by Danny Baker (2012)

Better than a Gun in a Knife Fight by A. Razor (2012)

The Daughters of Bastards by Iris Berry (2012)

Drawn Blood: Collected Works from D.B.P.Ltd., 1985-1995 by A. Razor (2012)

Impress by C.V. Auchterlonie (2012)

Tomorrow, Yvonne: Poetry & Prose for Suicidal Egoists by Yvonne De la Vega (2012)

Beaten Up Beaten Down by A. Razor (2012)

Miracles of the Blog: A Series (2012) by Carolyn Srygley-Moore (2012)

8th & Agony by Rich Ferguson (2012)

Untamed by Jack Grisham (2013)

Moth Wing Tea by Dennis Cruz (2013)

Half-Century Status by A. Razor (2013)

Showgirl Confidential by Pleasant Gehman (2013)

Blood Music by Frank Reardon (2013)

I Will Always Be Your Whore by Alexandra Naughton (2014)

A History of Broken Love Things by SB Stokes (2014)

Yeah, Well... by Joel Landmine (2014)

Dreams Gone Mad with Hope by S.A. Griffin (2014)

FORTHCOMING FROM PUNK HOSTAGE PRESS

When I Was a Dynamiter by Lee Quarnstrom (2014)

Stealing the Midnight from a Handful of Days by Michele McDannold (2014)

Dead Lions by A.D. Winans (2014)

Thugness Is a Virtue by Hannah Wehr (2014)

Where the Road Leads You by Diana Rose (2014)

Disgraceland by Iris Berry & Pleasant Gehamn (2014)

Introvert/Extrovert by Russell Jaffe (2014)

Shooting for the Stars in Kevlar by Iris Berry (2014)

Dangerous Intersections by Annette Cruz (2014)

Driving All of the Horses at Once by Richard Modiano (2014)

The Red Hook Giraffe by James Anthony Tropeano III (2014)

Visit www.punkhostagepress.com for further information about these and other available titles.

Made in the USA
Charleston, SC
13 April 2016